Dating The Other Color and His Mother

Do mothers always want what's best for you or what's best for them?

Jetta Whyte

iUniverse, Inc.
New York   Bloomington

Dating The Other Color and His Mother
Do mothers always want what's best
for you or what's best for them?

Copyright © 2009 Jetta Whyte

iUniverse books may be ordered through booksellers or by contacting:

iUniverse
1663 Liberty Drive
Bloomington, IN 47403
www.iuniverse.com
1-800-Authors (1-800-288-4677)

ISBN: 978-1-4401-5763-9 (pbk)
ISBN: 978-1-4401-5762-2 (ebk)

Printed in the United States of America

iUniverse rev. date: 9/18/09

To my husband: thank you for all your love and support through this journey.
I love you.

Contents

❖

Introduction

Let me first start by saying this is not a book that is based on a story about an interracial couple dating and facing the ignorance of their families, friends, and society as a whole. This is a book that is going to give women who are dating outside of their race the lowdown on how to deal with not only a mother who's jealous that her son is being taken away from her bosom, but a mother who's angry because she's losing her son to a woman of another race—a race that she may not be too fond of.

I went through this for six years before my husband and I got married. My husband's mother did not want me in her house. She would not talk to me or welcome me at family functions. In fact, she treated me inhumanly. For years and years, I had to put up with the rude, racial comments she would make about me as she denied me access to her house—even her guest bathroom. She did not even want my car in her driveway. Yes, shocking but all so true. And did I mention for six years I dealt with this? Yes, six years.

Oh, I mustn't forget to let you know that I am African American, and my husband is Cuban American. The fact that her son was dating an African American was definitely something she was not too fond of.

While going through this, I felt so lost, and I would constantly search for advice. I would even search for books and Web sites that would tell me how to deal with this unfortunate situation. Whenever I went to the bookstores, all I would find were fictional stories about interracial couples. The novels always had the same scenario: a black man dating a white woman and being bad-mouthed by other black women. Never did I find a self-help book to lend me realistic advice on what to do in certain situations I found myself in with his mother. I wanted to hear how other women in my same predicament had dealt with their respective "mothers." Did they confront them about their racism? Did they stand up for themselves in the face of disrespect? Or did they just ignore the ignorance.

I had to learn on my own how to deal with the ignorance of racism coming from the mother of the man I love. Believe me, it's not the same as dealing with the racism you encounter on the streets. If some random person makes a racial comment while you and your man are out to dinner, you would (without doubt) set that person straight. But you can't necessarily do that when dealing with the mother of the person you love. You have to show respect at all times (we will discuss this later). Respect for his mother is a must. So, I would love to share some of the realistic situations that I have been through with his mother, and, in the process, lend you some key advice on how to date the other color and his mother.

1

❖

I'm Qualified

What qualifies me to tell you how to deal with his mother? As I stated in the intro, I dealt with my husband's racist mother and all her drama and ignorance for six years before we married. So, I know exactly what you are going through. If you think I don't or if you think that what I went through isn't as bad as what you're going through, then sit back and let me briefly fill you in on my six years of racist torture. When I'm finished, you will certainly say I'm qualified.

When my husband and I met, I was nineteen. Through my entire life I had attended predominantly white schools, and I had played on predominantly white sports teams. I have been the only black girl in plenty of places. I was always invited to sleepovers and birthday parties and never had to deal with a single racial incident. That is, until I met my husband. Of course, the racism didn't come from him—the number one source was his mother.

My husband and I started dating during summer break. He went to school in Georgia and I was going to school right at home in Fort Lauderdale. You know, when there is someone you're dating who is really special to you, you want to take him home so your family can meet him. Well, that's not how it went for me. Yes, I took him to meet my family, but he did not take me to meet his family right away. It kind of freaked me out because I was thinking that maybe I wasn't special enough to him for him to want to take me home to meet his family. Or maybe I wasn't the only one he was dating. Everything was going through my head as I tried to figure out why he was not even hinting about taking me home to meet his family.

Whenever we would hangout, he would always come to my house. If I went to see him, we would go for walks in his neighborhood or I would leave my car at his parent's house and we would go to the movies or go get ice cream. But he would never invite me in. I knew that his mom knew about me because I frequently called his house and she would answer the phone and ask for my name.

We had probably been dating for two months when he finally told me why he had not taken me to meet his parents. One night, he came to my house, and I could tell something was wrong by the look in his eyes. He called me to meet him outside by his car. He looked worried, frustrated, sad, and confused. He couldn't even look into my eyes.

He started by saying, "I didn't know, but my parents are racist and they don't want me dating you." "*What!*" I said. In my naïveté I said, "How do you know they are racist? Maybe they just need to get to know me." He went on to tell me how his mom had said that he could do better than dating some black girl ... how he should date in his own race ... how there were plenty of Cuban girls for him ... blah blah blah. I believed that his mother was speaking for herself as well as for her husband. But, I got it: she didn't like me because I am black. But actually, I didn't get it. I was so naive, so optimistic, so fixed on "she has to get to know me" that I honestly didn't grasp the truth in what he was saying to me. I was also informed that because his mother didn't approve of him dating me, she didn't want me in her house. I had no idea of all the hurt and pain that was ahead me.

After that night, we had only about two more weeks together before he went back to school in Georgia. Yes, we did the long distance thing for the first two years of our relationship. I didn't get the true extent of this "racism" problem until he came back for Christmas break. By this time we had been dating for six months.

Cubans have a Christmas tradition called *Noche Buena*. It is celebrated on Christmas Eve, when families get together for food, drinks, and fun. Well, he told me that the party was being held at his grandparent's house, and I didn't have to ask; I knew I wasn't invited. Being so naïve made me not question why I wasn't invited because I figured, when a son or daughter goes away to school, the only opportunities for home and family visits are summer break, Thanksgiving break, Christmas break, and spring break. So, when he came home to visit his family, I never bugged him about spending all his time with me. I figured, when he came home for Thanksgiving or Christmas, that would be time for him to spend with his family. I didn't ask him to come to Thanksgiving dinner at my house because I knew he would want to be with his family. So, I did not throw a hissy fit about not being invited to Noche Buena; we just decided to meet up afterwards. He told me that he would call me around nine to let me know I could be on my way to his house. He called me at eight and said to come over. I asked him if the party was over already because it was so early, and he said, "No, but you can come now."

When I got to his neighborhood, I saw him running up the street. I open the passenger door to let him in, and, before he could close the door, he said (out of breath), "Turn around." Then he said, "I lied. Noche Buena was at my house." I said, "Why did you lie to me?" And he said, "Because I would have felt bad telling you that the party was at my house knowing that I couldn't invite you. So I said that it was at my grandparents' house." And that's when he broke down crying. He literally fell over in my lap while I was driving. He sobbed and sobbed. He continued to try to tell me the events of the night through his tears. First, his mother had tried to hook him up with her sister's friend. He told me how his father didn't want me there because it would send a bad message to my husband's younger sister—that it's okay for her to date a black guy. My future husband said that rude comments about him dating me had been made all night. He had finally had enough. I felt so bad for him. I had no idea what to say or do to make him feel okay because it wasn't okay. I just let him lie in my lap and cry. I finally realized how real this situation was.

For the next two and a half years, I was not allowed in his family's house. I could not even use the guest bathroom, at least while they were awake. There were times when I was desperate and couldn't make it to the all-too-familiar, nearby Shell gas station bathroom. His parents would be sleep, so he would sneak me in to use the bathroom. Then there were times—many times—when I had to act like a dog and pee in the bushes. Oh, wait, there was one time, two years into our dating, when I used the guest bathroom and it was okay by his mother. But he did have to call into the house and *ask* if it was okay before she said yes. In two years, that was the first time I had ever seen the inside of his house, because the lights were on. When he would sneak me in to use the bathroom, all the lights would be off! Plus, that was the first time his parents had seen my face. I felt as if that was my lucky night because I didn't have to play like a dog or go into a nasty gas station bathroom to pee. I had finally made my way in the house! Yay! While I was there, I finally met his mother and father. They played nice, but that was it. No more invites to use the guest bathroom. No invites to dinner. No invitations to watch TV. *Nothing* for the next year.

Eventually, our third anniversary popped around. By this time, my future husband had already transferred to a college in Florida, so we were seeing each other almost every day. But something didn't feel right—not with him, but with me. This whole situation was taking a toll on me; mentally and emotionally. All I could think about was how his mother didn't like me for something that I couldn't control. It's not as if I had a character flaw or

I had been rude or disrespectful to her. She didn't like me because of the color God made me. I would think about stories my friends shared with me about the good relationships they had with their boyfriends' moms, and I couldn't help but be jealous. My friends would tell me how they went to their boyfriends' house to watch TV, and all I could think was, "Wow, that must be nice. I can't do that because my boyfriend's mother doesn't like me because I'm black. We have to stay outside his house and sit in the driveway because I'm not allowed in the house."

I would think about how my future husband had such a great relationship with not only my mom, but with my entire family, and I couldn't help but be even more jealous. I thought about every single time I had had to use the bathroom outdoors or in a public restroom because they wouldn't allow me in their home. I thought about every time they had a family function and I wasn't invited.

Everything I had been through for the past three years was consuming my thoughts, and I couldn't help but feel disrespected and insulted. I would think, *Why am I putting myself through this? I love him and all, but I deserve better than being treated like this. I am a good girl, I'm educated, I work, I have goals—and she treats me like I'm some nasty girl off the streets who's out to hurt her son.* Plus, I felt he wasn't sticking up for me the way I thought he should (we will talk about that later). I had had enough, and I wrote him a letter that I will share with you.

The letter

I want to first apologize for the way that I have been the past few days. I honestly had so much on my mind that I shut down. A lot of the stuff on my mind has to do with the way I have been treated by your parents for the past three years. The way that I have been feeling has been going on for a long time, non-stop.

I know you thought everything was okay because you see me happy, smiling, and laughing. But, on the inside, I am so hurt and sad. I feel sad, hurt, discouraged, disrespected, unappreciated, not good enough, and angry. I am tired of feeling the way I feel. Three years tired. I have had enough. It has been a mental and emotional battle for me. Emotionally, I still cry. I am even out of tears. Mentally, I think about this every day. I think about what has happened in the past three years (you know, I don't forget anything). I think about how it has actually been three years and there are no signs of improvement. And I think about how that scares me for our future together.

I am sad and hurt because of how your parents treat me. They treat me as if I am a bad person who wants to hurt you. They treat me as if I have disrespected them or something. And I have put up with it for three years. They have done so many rude things to me. Everything from not allowing me in the house (like I'm trash), to not allowing me to use your guest bathroom so I have to pee outside (like a dog) or at gas stations, to hanging up on me when I call your house to speak to you, to trying to hook you up with other girls, to not even speaking to me when I go to your games. I have had it. They win. No one should feel the way I feel or be treated the way I have been treated just for loving you.

You would think that they would be happy for you that you found someone whom you love, someone who loves you, someone who makes you happy; but all they care about is that I'm black. But that is between you and your parents. I have realized that I cannot ask for their respect because you don't even have their respect. I hope one day you receive the respect you deserve as a man. But, until then, I cannot be involved in a situation like this. Actually, I do not deserve to be in a situation like this. I deserve to be treated with respect because all I ever did was love you. I deserve to date someone whose parents respect me and appreciate me for being someone who makes their son happy and who only wants the best for him. It hurts me so badly when one of my friends says that she went to her boyfriend's house to chill or watch a movie. I wish that was me. It also hurts me to see the way my family accepts you and loves you. My parents didn't see you as Cuban when you walked through the door; they saw what was important: that we loved each other and that you made me happy. I honestly don't think your parents care if you're happy, but that's not for me to judge.

I wish I could tell you what to do or say to get your parents to change and respect you, but I won't. That's all up to you. The advice I will give you is this: if you feel you cannot talk to your parents, then maybe you should write them a letter and tell them everything you feel.

I have run out of patience, and I have run out of hope. I'm sorry I fell weak, but anyone in my shoes would understand. And I know that I am not the only one hurting. I am sorry for everything your parents have put you through because of me. I love you so much, and I will always love you.

Love always and forever,

Jetta

Pretty bold letter, huh? Well guess who read it. Yep, his mother read the letter. He called me a day after and told me she had found it and read it. At first, I was so embarrassed, but then I was happy that she had read it and got a chance to see all that she had put me (us) through. So when he called and told me she'd read it, he also told me that she wanted to have lunch with me. So, I thought, *Wow, it took three years and a break-up letter to be invited to lunch! Who could have known?*

So, I took her up on lunch, and my husband tagged along. The lunch, of course, was awkward, and all she did was make excuses (she is the queen of excuses; you'll see) for how she had treated me for the past three years. Her excuses ran the gamut. At first, she thought I was influencing my husband to do bad things (she didn't elaborate because she'd made it all up). Then she was worried because her older son had married an American girl and she had left him with a child. I didn't understand what that excuse had to do with me. But just read on, the excuses get even more ridiculous.

Do you think I got an apology from her for how I had been treated for the past three years? A single "I'm sorry"? No, nothing … just a bunch of ridiculous, made-up excuses. In my reality, there are no excuses in the world to justify the way I had been treated. But, I gave her the benefit of the doubt. Understand, I had been praying for this day to come … a day when I could sit and talk to her and let her get to know me … a day when she could ask me whatever she wanted in order to get to know me. I was so excited. I thought this was going to be a new beginning for us. I was so grateful for that opportunity that I sent her a thank you card to show her how much I appreciated her meeting with me.

Her pretending to like me lasted for about two months. Yes, I said "pretending" because it was all fake (you'll see). During the two months, we had movie nights on Fridays at her house. She would also invite me to dinner, and I would bring the dessert. It was perfect. God had finally answered my prayers. Then the movie nights suddenly stopped, and my future husband didn't invite me to come over as much. And then one night I came to my future husband's parents' house to find his mother standing outside saying good-bye to his sister. So, I pulled into the driveway to park my car because we were taking my future husband's car. She didn't wait until I got out of my car so we could say hello. Instead, she turned around and literally speed walked into the house to avoid talking to me. It was so weird because two weeks earlier we had all been sitting on the couch having a movie night.

So I jumped in the car with my future husband and he mentioned it before I could. "I wonder why my mom ran in the house like that?" A few weeks went by, and I finally asked him why we hadn't gone to his house in a while. And he confirmed what I had been suspecting … that for some reason his mother didn't want me there anymore. He said that she told him that she couldn't get use to me (a black woman) walking around her house." Boy, did that hurt. I was devastated because I thought she liked me; I thought the racism was over. But it was back!

So I didn't go there for about nine months after that. It would have been longer, but my future husband broke his leg in a landscaping accident and was in the hospital for days. That was the first time I had seen her since the night when she had sprinted into the house to avoid talking to me. Of course, it was awkward seeing her at the hospital, but, honestly, I was not concerned about her at that moment; my concern was with my future husband. When he was being discharged from the hospital, he had to *ask* his mother if I was allowed to come to her house to see him while he recovered. It was so sad that he had to ask if his girlfriend of four years could come to the house to see him. Fortunately, she said yes.

Here is where I fell for her fake act once again. At the time, I still didn't recognize her smiles and kindness as fake. I guess you could say I didn't *want* to see her behavior as fake. You would think that I would have learned my lesson not to trust her, but I was still hopeful about the situation. I also thought that maybe she would talk to me and tell me what had happened before to make her not want me at movie nights anymore. Or maybe she would consider the fact that I loved her son so much, that I stayed by his side in the hospital every night to make sure he was okay; and all of that would make her like me again. But the truth is, she never liked me. I was only setting myself up for more devastation.

While I was helping him recuperate from his broken leg, I visited him at home almost every day for about two and a half months. On some days, his mother would say how she was happy that I was there to help, and on other days, she wouldn't say much to me at all other than an occasional "hi." But, of course, she never talked about why, all of a sudden, she hadn't wanted me at movie nights anymore. She just acted as if nothing ever happened (she is actually really good at sweeping things under the rug and pretending that she's innocent). She, in fact, never got into deep conversations with me. She never tried to get to know me while I was there. Actually, she did one time during the two and a half months that I was there, ask me about my job. But, once my future husband was well enough to drive, we were back to him coming to my house and me never being invited to his.

In January, three months after the accident that broke his leg, and four and a half years after we had begun dating, my future husband asked me to marry him. It was one of the happiest days of my life. Of course, I had to tell everyone I knew that I was engaged. My family was so happy for us, and our friends were so excited too. The situation with his mother and all her drama became invisible until friends and family who knew the situation started asking me if his mother knew about our engagement, then I started to wonder if he had told her.

About a week after he asked me to marry him, I asked him if his mom knew yet. He got so nervous at the mere mention of telling her. Do you know that he didn't even want to tell her? He wanted her to randomly find out. I told him that it would be even worse if she found out from someone else that he was getting married. Plus, I was not going to hide the fact that we were engaged as if I was ashamed or as if he was ashamed that he had asked me. I told him to call her and tell her that we were engaged to be married.

Oh, boy! All I heard, on the other end of the phone, was her saying that he was "making a big mistake." And "ya'll are going to have little black-and-white babies and those kids have problems all the time."

Yeah, because of people like you, was what I was thinking. I think he ended up hanging up on her. It put a little damper on our excitement, but what did we expect from someone who had given us grief throughout our whole relationship? So we got over it and started planning our wedding.

That was in January, and I didn't go back to my future husband's house until July, when I waited for him for about twenty minutes while he changed clothes after a baseball game. His sister, mom, and dad were there. Only his sister spoke to me. She has always been very sweet to me and accepting of my relationship with her brother. But his father and the mother put on the fake smiles because "Jetta's in the house." That's how it's always been, "Jetta's in the house, let's pretend like we like her." Sad but true. It's a horrible feeling (a feeling I know too well) to be around people who smile in your face, but can't stand the skin you're in.

Let me tell you about the drama I caused by attending his nephew's birthday party that September. I showed up at the party, and it was the same as any other party I had been allowed to attend. Actually, no, it wasn't. There was lots of tension in the air at this party, and I knew for sure I was not supposed to be there. I walked in, and his father said hello to me and told me to come and eat. So I fixed my plate, but I didn't see my fiancé's mother anywhere.

I decided to eat outside because all of the inside tables were taken. As I walked outside, I saw her coming into the house. She saw me and just gave me a "Hi, Jetta" and kept on walking. I said, "Hi" and kept heading outside. That was all she said to me the entire night. Don't get me wrong, I didn't want her to focus all her attention on me, but I was her son's fiancé—his future wife and her future daughter-in-law. I mean, give me more than just a walk-by "Hi."

So, the drama didn't happen that night. The drama happened the next day when she exploded at my future husband for inviting me to the party without her permission. From that point on, I swore to him that I would never set foot in that house again, and I didn't care if I never saw his mother again. I was definitely angry, and had the right to be. She was playing games with me. One minute she supposedly liked me and wanted me to come over for movie nights. Then she, all of a sudden, didn't like me and didn't want me in her home. But when my future husband got hurt and needed someone to assist him, it was okay for me to come into the house. And there we were again, back at square one—she didn't want me around unless she invited me. I had every right to be upset, and, by this time, I did not trust her one bit. How could I trust someone who kept going back and forth, playing with my emotions? I didn't go back to his house until he had the second surgery on his leg, which was that December.

Brace yourself for this one. This is when I realized that people will say and do whatever they can to get whatever they want. In this case, I realized his mother would say whatever she could to avoid admitting that it's the color of my skin that made her treat me the way she did.

The morning of his surgery, his parents decided that they wanted to take me to breakfast to kill some time. Lord knows, I didn't want to go anywhere with her. I had brought a magazine and just planned on waiting it out in the waiting room. I didn't even plan on talking to her or anything, especially after her rampage about me coming to the birthday party that she hadn't invited me to. So, I didn't want to be rude; I went along with them to breakfast. *Big mistake!*

While we were at breakfast, his mother had the nerve to ask me why I didn't come inside the house when I came to see her son anymore. (Remember, I hadn't been back inside her house since the birthday party incident, which was three months prior to this breakfast. And when I did go there, I waited for him in my car. And a couple of times she had come outside and seen me waiting for him). I could not believe she asked me that. Here she goes again sweeping what she'd done under the rug and acting as if she was innocent.

I had to ask her to repeat the question because I was so blown away that she was acting so clueless. She tried to act as if she was oblivious as to why I didn't come inside her house; as if she hadn't thrown a fit the last time I came inside. I told her I had been told I was not welcome in her home. She looked like a deer caught in headlights; she obviously hadn't expected me to say that. Of course, she went on to blame it on her son, saying, "He misinterpreted my words."

Let's pause for a minute. I need some help here. Can someone please tell me how you misinterpret, "I don't want that black girl in this house"? That seems like a pretty clear statement to me ... or did she mean to say, "I don't want her here on Tuesdays"? I don't get it; I never understood any of her excuses because they were always lame and weakly thrown together ... like something she just made up on the spot. But that was her trying really hard to make up something or look for someone to blame so she wouldn't have to admit her own faults. Then she started her little game again by telling me that now I was welcome at her house. All I could think was, *How long this time before I'm not allowed on the premises again? Two weeks? One month? Maybe three months ...* I just let her talk and say what ever she wanted; I knew I'd be a fool to believe anything she said. But that isn't even the bombshell.

After breakfast, we got back in the car, and my future husband's father stopped at the gas station. While the father was out pumping gas, the mother and I were alone. She started to tell me the craziest, made-up, manipulative story *ever*. I won't get into grave detail, but she not only insulted my sexuality, but the sexuality of her own son. She pretty much told me she thought that our relationship was one big cover. Thank God I can laugh now, but, I didn't laugh then. I was actually in shock. I honestly stared at her, speechless, for a full minute, as if she was crazy. I couldn't believe what I was hearing. I was so insulted that she would think the last six years and our engagement were a cover to hide our true sexuality (that we were both gay). I was floored that she would think my husband was using me and our relationship as a front, so no one would suspect anything.

Do you see the distance she was willing to go? I maintained my cool and simply told her that her idea was ridiculous. Her story was that she had gone onto my MySpace page and had seen a picture of me and one of my friends hugging and blowing kisses at the camera (you know—the pose you take with all your friends when you're out partying). Well, she took that picture and misconstrued it to be something that it totally was not. And did I mention she made this harsh judgment of her son and I from one single picture? Yes, she didn't bother to look at the other 499 pictures I have in my profile and see that I'm not bear hugging all my girlfriends as if I'm in love with them. Not even that, she didn't bother to consider that her son and I had been together for six years. I like to take silly, funny pictures sometimes. And a picture of me blowing kisses at the camera and hugging a friend doesn't quite qualify as a picture that would make you question my sexuality. She found a picture she thought she could use in her defense of her dislike for me, when really all she did was make herself look incredibly foolish and made the situation even worse. I was flabbergasted and knew that, if she would say that about her own son (forget me), she would stop at nothing.

She only told me this crazy story because she wanted to come up with another excuse for why she didn't want me in her home (she should have just left it at my future husband "misinterpreting her words"; that was silly enough). And, after telling me this crazy story, she said, "Don't tell him I said that, I don't need the drama." She doesn't need the drama? That's all she has given us is *drama*!

At the beginning of this chapter, I told you that I am qualified to write this book. Now, after reading my story, you can tell me if I'm qualified or not.

2

---　❖　---

Demand Respect, but be Gentle in the Pursuit of It

I know in the first chapter I mentioned something about my future husband not sticking up for me the way I wanted him to. Well, it's true; he did not stick up for me the way I felt he should. He would sit there and listen to his mother say racist things about me, and he wouldn't say anything. He'd just walk away from her as if that was making enough of a statement. For example, my future husband came home late from visiting me one night and left his parents' garage door open. The next day, when his parents were leaving for work, they found it open and blew a gasket. His father woke my future husband up screaming normal things like, "Things could have been stolen!" and "Someone could have come in the house through the garage and robbed all of us!" But, do you want to know what his mother screamed at him? "That black girl is driving you crazy! You need to find someone who's going to give you peace and tranquility!" So, of course, his leaving the garage door open was the "black girl's" fault. But when she said all of that, do you know what my future husband did to defend me? *Nothing!* He just rolled over and went back to sleep.

For a long time, that's what he did. He would just walk out or go to his room when she was on one of her rampages about me. And I would get so mad at him for not standing up for me. I would wonder, *How is leaving the room when she is disrespecting me standing up for me?* It wasn't; at least it wasn't to me. I wanted him to tell her to leave me alone and stop blaming me for things I didn't do, but she would always get mad at him and start bad-mouthing me. I have yet to understand the logic behind that.

First, let me start by saying that the way your man sticks up for you, and how much he sticks up for you, is strongly dependent upon whether he lives with his parents or on his own. My husband lived with his parents up until two months before we got married. So for the entire six years that we were dating, he lived under their roof and their rules.

So what is a man to do when he is stuck between the woman that he loves (you) and a mother who is constantly on his case for being with you because your race isn't good enough for her? First, let's get the easy part out of the way. If your man does not live at home with his racist mother, then you've got it good and so does he. He doesn't have to listen to his mother twenty-four/seven insulting you and nagging him about being with you. This, in turn, can become very stressful for him and cause a huge stress on your relationship (trust me, I know). Since he doesn't live at home with her, he doesn't have to deal with her lack of respect for him. A lack of respect is exactly what it is when his mother says insulting things about you in his presence. We will discuss this more later.

My husband use to hate to go home. He would purposely stay at my house late so that, when he got home, his mother would be sleep. Sad, huh? Plus, if your man lives on his own, you don't have to worry about seeing his mother all the time. And I know how stressful that can be. It's the most awful feeling to be somewhere around a group of people and know your presence is not wanted. Ever since I have been allowed in his parents' house, I have never been comfortable there. Even when they are not there, I still feel an unpleasant aura. It's weird but it's true; I am very uncomfortable in that house. I think it's because I know of all the many fights and arguments that have taken place in that house over me.

When your man lives on his own, you can go to the peace and quiet of his motherless home and be relaxed. Don't get me wrong, I'm not trying to say that you ladies with boyfriends who live on their own don't have it bad, or to say that you are not going through torture also. But it is totally different when your man lives right under his parents' roof; it's so much more stressful.

Now, I'm going to concentrate on the ladies who have men who still live under their parents' roof. First, be understanding and be patient with the way he handles the situation. Remember, this is his family. He can't just curse them out and send them to hell. At first, I was not understanding. I wanted respect and I wanted it done my way. I felt his way of defending me wasn't good enough. In all my selfishness, I failed to understand his circumstances and his way of handling different situations.

All throughout our relationship when I heard that he hadn't stood up for me (my way) when she disrespected me, we would fight and I would tell him that I was hurt that he hadn't "done" anything. But he *was* fighting for me—in his own way. Whenever his mother said something slick about me, he would defend me, but, to protect my feelings, he didn't tell me every time they fought because he didn't want to tell me about the hurtful things she had said to start the fight.

His way of proving to her that her words meant nothing was to shut her out of his life. He barely talked to her about anything. He stopped going to family get-togethers and even Thanksgiving dinners. He was showing her that, no matter what she could say about me, he was still going to love me. So, he did fight for me—just not in the way that I wanted him to. I wanted him to do drastic things like leave, move out, put his foot down, put her in her place, stop talking to her, or stop going on vacations with her. I realized I was being selfish and wanted things done my way.

I also didn't give much consideration to his circumstances. I didn't realize that he was going through way more than I was. He was in love for the first time in his life to a wonderful woman (me) and he didn't have the support of his mother, the person who is supposed to love and support him unconditionally. He had to live with his mother who was constantly disrespecting him by saying racial things about me and making unnecessary hurtful comments about our relationship. One time, she told him that he thought he was black because he was always with me and my family. There was even a time that she told him that if he stayed with me she would take him out of her will. Unbelievable? Well, believe it. This is what he had to put up with daily.

If your man does fight for you, then good; at least he is not rolling over like a dog, sending his parents the message that they can do and say whatever they want about you. He is letting them know that you are worth fighting for. Even though he may not be standing up for you the way you want him to, he is still standing up for you.

My best advice to you is not to push him too hard about standing up for you. Like I said, he is *stuck* between you and his mother. You don't want him to think that you are making him turn against his mother because you would never want to make him think that. If you're constantly telling him, "Why didn't you say anything?" "Why didn't you stand up for me?" "When are you going to stand up for me?" or even, "That's all you said to her?" then he is going to feel pressured or as if he isn't doing what he should be doing as a man. You are basically criticizing him, and men feel belittled by criticism. He will also feel unappreciated by you and will start to think it's not worth sticking up for you and getting into battles with his mother if all you're going to do is tell him it's not good enough. Believe me, we had this fight all the time. He would confide in me about how he and his mother had gotten into a fight because she had said something rude about me, and I would spend the whole night asking him why he hadn't stood up for me the way I wanted him to. I would tell him over and over that the way he did stand up for me sucked. He would eventually shut down and want to run away from me. I now know that he was only coming to me so I could tell him, "Thank you for standing up to her." And here I was criticizing him for how he did it and telling him what he should have done.

Every time your man does defend you, thank him and let him know that you appreciate his efforts on your behalf. If you show him that you are appreciative of his efforts, he will stand up for you more often. Make your man feel like a *man*; don't annoy him about the situation. Trust me, he knows the faults of his mother and he will stand up for you in his own way.

Remember, he is defying his own mother to be with you; in some cases, he is defying his entire family. In my case, it wasn't just my husband's mother. Yes, she was the ringleader and the main one throwing racial bombs, but his paternal grandparents were also involved. When we had been dating for a few years, my future husband told me his grandfather told him that he was disgracing his father by dating me. There was also an incident when his grandparents were throwing a party and we thought it was okay for us both to go (that's what we had been told), so we went. When his grandmother saw us pull up to the front of the house, she started clearing the table of all the food, screaming, "The party is over!" My husband's aunt was also there, saying, "Who invited him? You knew he would bring that black girl!" I was so hurt, and I could tell my husband was too. So, it wasn't just the ignorance of his mother he had to deal with.

My husband always told me his father never really cared that he was dating me—it was more his mother who didn't want him with me. I just don't understand; if his dad didn't care that he was dating me, why didn't he try to talk some sense into her? Who knows?

My whole point is, cut your man some slack. He is risking a lot to be with you. My husband pretty much risked being disowned by his family. He sacrificed his relationship with his mother to be with me. It took me years to realize how much he was sacrificing for me; and once I did, I let him know how grateful I was.

Don't get me wrong, I still needed him to stand up for me every time something slick came out of his mother's mouth. I'm not telling you to totally lay off him. If your man is saying nothing to defend you from his mother, then I consider that a huge problem. He is either scared to stand up for you or he doesn't think you are worth the trouble. It's all about respect, and your man may not have the respect of his mother. He could be scared to state his opinion or what he believes in (your relationship). Sorry to say, but he has to grow some balls and say something—if not for you, then for himself. If he cares about you, then he will stand up to anyone who disrespects you, even his mother.

In the beginning of our relationship, my husband wasn't very quick to stand up for us because his parents didn't respect his opinion. My husband will even admit he wasn't allowed to have an opinion in his parents' home. In that house, he was still considered a little boy, and they didn't care about how he felt or what he thought. To show him how much respect his mother had for him, she would say nasty things about me right in front of him or make racial comments while he was in her presence.

I would ask him why he didn't demand respect from his mother. He would say that he did, but I knew he didn't. I told him he should let his mother know that when she disrespected the woman he loved (me), right in front of him, she was also disrespecting him. Well, he told her that and she told him that, if he didn't like it, he could leave. Can you believe that? You don't even know how many times his parents threatened to kick him out. They'd rather kick him out than give him the respect he deserved as a man. I understand he still lived under their roof, but does that mean he was not allowed to have an opinion? Does that mean he wasn't entitled to respect? Under their roof or not, he still deserved respect as a human being. All he was asking was for them to show him respect by not disrespecting his girlfriend in his presence. One day they threatened to kick him out and he finally left. The best day of my life!

If he says that he loves you, then he should want to protect you from the harsh words of his mother or his family. Plus, if he believes in your relationship, then he should stand up for what he believes in. If he doesn't have the courage to demand respect for not only you, but for himself, then you will never get the respect you deserve. Keep in mind that you will not get the respect you deserve until he gets the respect he deserves. How will they respect you when they don't even respect him? As I said earlier, it wasn't until after we were married and he had moved out of his parents' house that my husband received the full respect that he deserved as a man from his parents. Don't give up hope, just be patient.

My advice is not to push him too much. Let him stand up for you in his own way. But make sure that he is saying something in your defense. If he doesn't, then you have a problem. Also, acknowledge when he does stand up for you, and let him know how much you appreciate it. Ever since I started to tell my husband how proud I was of him for what he had said or done in my defense, he started defending me more. These days, if his mother were to even look at me crazy, he would be ready to run to my defense.

3

❖

Heads Up

This chapter is actually hilarious to me even though I know the situations I present aren't a bit funny. However, I could never help but crack up at how desperate his mother was to break us up. This chapter is totally dedicated to helping you become aware of some of the tricks and plots your man's mother may try in order to break you two up or cause problems in your relationship. I can honestly say I—well … we—fell for all of them. So, take notes on how not to become a victim like I was.

"I Had a Dream"

This one is funny; she got us with this one a couple of times.

When his mother didn't know how to ask us certain questions, she would pretend she had "a dream" about the subject in question to get us to give her an answer. If you're confused, let me give you a few examples that fooled us.

My husband and his father have the same name, and one night my husband came home to find that some of his mail had been opened. One of those open envelopes contained a document about a condo that he had just bought but hadn't told his parents about. A couple of days later, his mother said to him, "I had a dream that you were moving out." At the time, we hadn't caught on to her manipulation, so he responded, "Really, that's weird because I can't afford to move out." So, she received the answer she was looking for. He wasn't, at the time, moving out. But, I guess she didn't believe him because when I came over that day to visit him, she felt it necessary to tell *me* about her "dream" also. I guess she wanted to see if our answers matched up, but I told her also that he wasn't moving out. That wasn't the only way she would use her "I had a dream" trap.

Back when we were dating she would occasionally tell my husband that she'd had a dream that I was pregnant—just to see what he would say. Whenever she suspected anything of us, instead of just asking him, she would tell him she'd had a dream about it to see what kind of response my husband would give her. That's another reason why it's so hard for me to trust her. Finally, a conversation with one of my friends opened my eyes to what his mother was doing. My friend was the one who told me his mother was only fishing for answers, and the only way she knew how to get them, because my husband never told her anything anymore, was to say she'd had "a dream" about whatever she was curious about and see what response she got.

So, the last time she talked to me (literally), she started telling me all this weird stuff about how she may not be that close to her children, but that she has "dreams" to give her signs as to what's going on in their lives. Are you thinking what I'm thinking? Anyway, I knew exactly where she was going, and I was ready this time. *Here she goes.* "Last night I had a dream you were pregnant." So, she paused and stared at me as if she was waiting for me to give her some sort of answer or reaction. I just stared at her as if to say, "yeah, and … " She saw that I was not giving her any response so she started adding on to the story saying "Oh, and I think it was a little boy." Then she paused again, waiting. But I gave her nothing but a blank stare. Finally she went on to change the subject. I wasn't about to let her manipulate me into giving her information with that "I had a dream" scheme.

I don't know if your boyfriend's mother uses this method, but just be aware of this little trick to get info from you. Only give her information you want her to know, when you want her to know it—not when she goes fishing for it.

Faking It

You've already read in this book about a lot of situations when my husband's mother pretended she liked me. This is an issue I am so familiar with, and you will see a lot more about it in this book. "Jetta's in the house, so let's pretend like we like her."

It's not as if I wanted my husband's mother to be rude to my face, because that would be the alternative to her smiling in my face and acting as if everything was okay. Let's just keep it real: she didn't like me and I knew it. On my part, I don't pretend that I like someone when I really don't, but at the same time I'm not rude. I say, "Hi, how are you?" and that's it. For years, I let my husband's mother get away with smiling in my face as if the way she treated me was okay. She would say nice things to me, and I would give her the benefit of the doubt. While I was in her presence, she wanted me to think she was a nice person, and for a while I did. I realized that her niceness was fake every time she allowed me into her home, then turn around and shut me out again. I figured she would continue smiling in my face as long as I let her because I wasn't calling her out on it. That was, until after my husband and I were married and I received my second "fake apology" (I'll tell you about the first one later) and I gave her the benefit of the doubt. Yes, again. But this time I played it smart; I told her straight up I did not trust her. I refused to treat her the way she treated me. I wasn't going to walk in her house all jolly, pretending that I was happy to see her the way she pretended with me. I gave her a "Hi, how are you?" and that was it.

But after I told her I didn't trust her and I wasn't going to be fake and pretend that I did, her phony act stopped—completely. She knew I had caught on to her fake act, and I wasn't falling for it any longer. Honestly, she went from being all smiles (fake) when she saw me to only "Hi, Jetta" and that's it—no fake "we're happy to see you," no fake "you look pretty today." Nothing. But, hey, that's fine with me. It was much better than when she pretended to like me and acted as if everything was okay.

If your man's parents started out treating you poorly and never gave you an apology, then don't trust their smiles. A sincere apology is the difference between a fake smile and a sincere one. Don't be fooled when his mother comes to you with a big smile, saying "you look pretty." If she hasn't apologized yet, it's fake. Treating people horribly because of the color of their skin is not the kind of issue that can be swept under the rug. You deserve a sincere apology, and a fake smile won't cut it.

Just don't follow in his mother's fakeness as I did for years. Yes, be kind to her. But realize that being kind to her doesn't mean you have to be fake (see chapter 6 for a more elaborate explanation). Give her a genuine "Hi, how are you?" You don't owe it to her to act as if you're happy to see her. Give her what she is entitled to as your boyfriend's mother until you get what you're entitled to—a sincere apology.

Stealing Your Time

My husband is the one who told me about this one; I had no clue. I thought the times he said he was going to dinner with his parents were planned, but I found that's not quite how it was.

When he would say he was coming to my house to visit me then turn around and call me an hour or two later saying, "Oh, I forgot my parents invited me to dinner," I would think he had just forgotten he had dinner plans with his parents before making plans with me (I guess he did make it seem that way … jerk). But this is how it really went: His mother would see him getting ready to leave the house—to come see me, of course—and she would go to him and say, "Oh, we were going to invite you to come to dinner with us." My husband, like most men, is a sucker for food (she knew exactly how to get him). So, he would end up canceling with me to go to dinner with his parents, which is fine, just sneaky on her part.

My husband said she would see him preparing to leave and make up something to get him to stay home. He said it ranged from, "Can you help your father with …" or "We're ordering dinner. What can I order you?" Anything to keep him home, basically stealing my time with him.

If this happens to you, which I'm sure it will because she can't stand the fact that he chooses to spend time with you rather than her, there is really nothing you can do about it. If he doesn't catch on to what his mother is doing, like my husband eventually did, don't point it out to him. Don't go to him saying, "Have you noticed whenever you're on your way to come see me, your mother always has something for you to do or all of a sudden wants to invite you to dinner?" This one he has to find out on his own because you don't want to seem possessive or as if you're keeping him from his family. The only time I would say to mention it to him is if he persistently cancels his dates with you because of her. Other than that, if it's once or twice, here and there, let him spend time with his mother.

Now, I know what I'm about to say will be a toughie, but I feel obligated to say it. Suggest he spend time with his mother. Tell him to take his mother to dinner or lunch. There was a time that my husband wanted to take his parents and I to dinner (this was after we were engaged) and his mother had the biggest hissy fit, saying, "If she goes, then we're not going." I guess she thought saying that would make him leave me at home and take her to dinner instead. But she was surprised (and the dinner was great!). After he told me what had gone down when he asked his parents to go, I told him it was okay, to go ahead and take his parents to dinner. And he was the one who said, "Absolutely not! If they can't have dinner with you, then they don't need to go." Even now, I tell him to take his parents to dinner, and he says, "I'm not going if you're not going."

Don't be selfish with him and never intentionally keep him from his family. In the long run, he may resent you if you do. Plus, telling him to take his parents to dinner or lunch can work in your favor if it's ever said that you're "separating" him from his family. That's what was said about me (I'll tell you about that later). My husband as my witness, I do encourage him to spend time with his parents. It's not my fault he doesn't want to go; all I can do is encourage it. And that's all you can do too.

I know that you may be thinking, "I could never tell him to go to dinner with his mother. She will probably bad-mouth me the entire time." Just do it. Do it for your man. He will appreciate you for it in the long run. And, hopefully, he will mention to his mother that having dinner was your suggestion. She won't know what to say about that.

Pretending to Like You When She Needs Something

Oh boy! This is a good one.

So one day his mother barely whispers a word to you and the next, she wants to take you to dinner. Has the apology come yet? No? Well, sorry to rain on your parade, but something is up. Pretending she liked me when she needed something is too familiar to me. One time when my husband was in the hospital with his broken leg and his mom took me to eat in the cafeteria, she tried to convince me to tell my husband to change his career path. Mind you, this is after not talking to me for about six months. But now, all of a sudden, she needed my assistance in convincing my husband to change his career. Funny.

His parents had been bugging him for months to stop doing landscaping and get a nine-to-five office job. His landscaping accident just gave his parents more reasons to convince him he shouldn't do landscaping. Well, my husband loved landscaping and actually now has a very successful landscaping business. I was not going to tell him to stop doing what he loves to do, and I told her that. Plus, his career is his decision. Once I told her that, she was ready to go. Her attempt had failed. At the end, I realized she only wanted to buy me dinner because she needed my help.

Then, a year later, there was the breakfast from hell (remember when she insulted both my and my husband's sexuality? Yeah, that breakfast). That morning, she only took me to breakfast to tell me that I was, all of a sudden, welcome in her home. She pretended to like me and acted as if everything was okay. Well, she was only putting up that phony act because she wanted my help to take care of my husband while he was recovering. She wanted me to help him shower, fix him something to eat when he was hungry, help him to the bathroom—pretty much get him whatever he needed. There was only one time, in the whole two months I was there helping him recover, when she said how happy she was that I was there helping out. But, after his recovery and after she had used me for what she needed me for, she was back to her same old ways.

People who don't like you and treat you horribly then refuse to apologize always have an ulterior motive when they, all of a sudden, want to be nice and sweet to you. But then they want to, all of a sudden, be nice to you.

Hmm ... makes you think something's up. Don't fall for it, because something *is* up. I just wish I knew back then what I know today. I learned my lesson. Just be careful.

Making You Jealous

This one is funny—well in my situation it was.

So, the first time my husband was in the hospital with his broken leg, he received flowers and phone calls from everyone he knew. After his surgery, they wheeled him back from the recovery room to his room, and his mother and father were already there waiting. Well, his mother started telling him some girl named Tisha had called him to see how he was doing. While she was telling him this, I could see her cutting her eyes over to me to see if I had some sort of reaction to some girl named Tisha calling my man. So she said it again because he didn't hear her. And this time when she repeated it, she looked directly at me to make sure I heard her also (hilarious). I just acted clueless, as if I didn't know this Tisha person, but actually I did. She is the wife of my husband's good friend. But his mother thought that maybe it was a girl he was probably talking to on the side, and the girl was calling to check up on him (her wishful thinking). She was basically trying to make me feel jealous that another woman was calling him. But, as I said, what she didn't know was that I knew the woman already. Plus, let me remind you, she was trying to pull this little stunt just as he was getting back from surgery. The things she did were so funny, but so sad at the same time.

When your boyfriend's mother starts to bring up old girlfriends or any other girl right in front of you to try to make you jealous, don't even sweat it (seriously). This is only her being vindictive and mean. It's just another desperate attempt to piss you off and start a fight between you and her son. Seriously, laugh her off. When she realizes you aren't intimidated or bothered by her malicious game (she'll probably get pissed), she'll leave it alone. When I didn't give her the reaction she was looking for and went on catering to my injured man, she eventually let it go because I simply ignored her. Her silly plan of trying to get me jealous didn't work.

You have to just ignore her and know that she is just being spiteful. If his mother says to him something like, "Susie called for you earlier," while you're sitting there, just smile at her. Yeah, deep down inside your wondering, *Who the heck is Susie, and why is she calling my man?* But don't let his mother know that. If she suggests to her son in front of you that he take you to a restaurant that he took his ex girlfriend to, just stay calm, smile and say something like, "Yeah, we went there and the food was so good." or "Yeah, we want to go there. I heard it's really nice." She will probably look at you crazy thinking, *Girl, didn't you just hear me say that he took his ex girlfriend there?* Like I said, it may piss you off a little that she brought up his ex, but that's what she's trying to do. Don't give her the satisfaction of letting her know she's getting to you. Be strong. This subject brings me to my next topic. Keep reading.

Not In Front of Her

Never let her know that one of her malicious plans to break you two apart is working or has caused you two to fight. Actually, scratch that. Just never let her know you two are fighting. That's her ammo.

My husband's mother saw us fighting once, and she still brings it up to this day. One Christmas my husband and I had just gotten back from Michigan. We decided to go to his parents' house to exchange gifts, and my husband's sister and brother were also there. My husband was telling his brother and sister about our trip to Michigan, and we were all laughing and having a nice time (one of few at that house). So his mother came out of nowhere and said to my husband, "Yeah, I remember the last time you two went to Michigan. Ya'll got into a big fight and she threw all your luggage in the yard and threw you out of the car."

First of all, she was definitely over exaggerating. Second, yes we did fight (who doesn't occasionally), but

I didn't throw either his luggage or him out of the car. He simply got out of the car (no one pushed him) and put (not threw) his luggage in the grass next to the car. The only reason she knew that we had been fighting was because, when he got out of the car, he slammed the door, and, when he took his luggage out of the trunk, he slammed the trunk. She didn't hear us yelling at each other or anything; she just figured he was slamming doors so we must be fighting.

Yes, I did set her straight (nicely) and told her that I hadn't thrown any of his things out of my car. Even my husband became angry and told her, "No one pushed me out of any car." She had totally ruined the mood, so we left right after that. When we got in our car, I was so mad, but I didn't say a word. My husband was the one who brought it up, saying, "Why did my mom need to bring that up? She saw that everyone was having a good time. Why would she bring up the time that we were fighting?"

Even if you and your man are in the biggest fight ever, never let her know anything. She will either add fuel to the fire or she will never let you live it down. My husband's mother thought she could bring that incident up as a humorous story when really my husband and I didn't want it to be part of a Christmas get together. Quite frankly, it was and still is none of her business.

Honestly, when she brought it up she was the only one laughing. All the other guests had that "wow, this is kind of awkward" look on their faces.

Whenever you and your man are fighting and she is around, act as if you're the happiest couple. It's a joy to her to see you two not getting along.

Convincing Him You're Not Good Enough

This is another one my husband came up with.

He told me about some of the things (not all of them, I'm sure) his mother told him to convince him I wasn't good enough for him (in actuality, that I was not good enough for her). Well, you know I like to throw my real-life examples at you, so here's one. My husband told me about one of the many times she tried to convince him of all of the reasons he should not be with me, and the subject of our future children came up (*huge* mistake on her part). She told him, "If you have children with her, your children wont be full Cuban!" She wanted him to marry a Cuban girl who would give him (and her) Cuban babies. This is funny to me as I'm writing it.

If your man's mother is always trying to tell him things to convince him not to be with you and he is still with you, then be thankful. You have a man who thinks for himself and doesn't let the ignorant words of his mother cloud his mind. Appreciate that because there are so many "momma's boys" out there who don't have minds of their own and who listen to every single thing their mommas tell them even if they make no sense. If there are any guys reading this book, sorry to say this, but most women are more mentally independent than some men. Hey, just keeping it real. All I'm saying is, think for yourself. That goes for everyone in all situations. If someone tells me a bunch of negative things about someone, I'm not going to automatically believe it all. I am going to find out on my own about that person and form my own opinion. I'm so grateful that my husband did not listen to all the negative things his mother was trying to fill his head with about me. He knew me better than she ever will. I hope she realizes now how much time and energy she wasted. But, in the process, she revealed how racist and judgmental she is.

Hopefully, you don't have a momma's boy; actually, I doubt very seriously that you have a momma's boy because he would have listened to his momma and left you a long time ago. Applaud your mentally independent man. I applaud mine.

Finding Info on You To Use Against You

Be careful about what you put out for the world to see— you know, MySpace, Facebook, and blog Web sites.

I told you about my MySpace incident. I still don't know how she got onto my MySpace page when it's private, but she did. Some mothers like to try to find any and everything to use against you. Even though the picture my husband's mother saw was so innocent, she made it out to be the nastiest picture she had ever seen. You would have thought I was actually kissing the girl in the picture instead of blowing kisses at the camera. (I can't help but laugh). I think, if his mother could—if she hasn't already—she would do a full-out background check on me to check for drug or murder charges I might be hiding. Just be careful, she could be watching you when you think she isn't. I'll say it again, don't give her anything to use against you. Be cautious.

4

❖

My Children

My husband and I haven't had the privilege of having children yet. We're hoping it will happen soon. But we have definitely had plenty of conversations about how we will handle the children situation when it comes to his family, especially his mother. Let me first say that I am very family oriented. I have loved to be around family ever since I was a little girl. I think I am this way because my parents always took us to visit family everywhere from Florida to Michigan. They felt it necessary for us to get to know both mom's side and dad's side of the family. Growing up as a little girl, I lived in Virginia, so we would pack up the car and have a family road trip to Florida for the summer and then another one in Michigan for the Christmas holidays.

Because of the way I was raised, so family oriented, I think it is extremely important for our children to know both sides of our family (his side and mine), especially since our cultures are so different. As I mentioned before, I am African American and he is Cuban American. Of course, we can enlighten our children with wonderful Cuban and African American culture and history, but we would also love the input of other family members. When my husband tells me things about Cuba, he tells me that he learned about them from his grandfather. When he cooks Cuban cuisine, he tells me that his grandmother taught him how. My husband was born in America, and Spanish is his first language because his grandparents babysat him when he was a little boy, and all they speak is Spanish. So he heard the Spanish language all day from them, and that's how he learned. It is extremely important to me that my children learn both cultures. I wish things were different because I would love for my children to be close to both sides of their family. There's not a doubt in our minds that our children will be loved, adored, and accepted by my family. So that's not the issue. The issue is, what do we do with his family and our children; mainly, what do we do with his mother?

Now, here are the questions and answers I'm sure you're dying to hear. Will I allow my husband's mother to be a part of our children's life? Of course I will. Would

I ever leave my children alone with her? Absolutely not! Whenever she and my husband's father want to see our children, we will bring them to their home or his parents will come visit us. I would never keep her from her grandchildren. As I said, I think it is absolutely necessary for our children to know both sides of the family. We are not particularly concerned with my husband's grandparents or other non immediate family members spending time with our children. We figure the non immediate family will see our children whenever we go to visit (which is not very often). We are more concerned with his mother.

It all boils down to trust, and, after all that I have been through with her, I don't trust her at all. But that's just me, and I have made my decision based on my situation and my gut. It wasn't as if I went through a couple of isolated incidents of his mother making racial comments or doing something really grimy to me. She treated me horribly for six years straight because of the color of my skin. From that, I know how she truly feels about me. It's obvious, if someone treats you nasty for years and years, then that treatment has to reflect his or her true feelings about you. That's how I look at it. How am I supposed to trust her with my children when I don't trust her with me? I'm sure you're wondering how my husband feels about my decision regarding our kids and his mother;

well he is 110 percent behind me. Let me add that I am not the only one who has trust issues with her. She has put a damper on my husband's trust toward her also. She has said and done a lot of hurtful things to him over the years, things that should never happen between mothers and their children. Many times my husband called me in a totally upset frame of mind saying that he couldn't believe what his mother had just said to him. He felt his mother should have loved and supported him no matter whom he chose to love. Since she didn't support him and his choice to love me, and since she treated us the way she did, the result is that now she has a son who doesn't look at her the way she would like him to. He has less respect for her than she would like. I'm telling you, six years of someone treating you the way she has treated us causes serious damage. And we don't think she realizes the hurt she has caused and the scars she has left behind from all that she has done.

My biggest fears are that she will treat my children differently from her other grandchildren ... that she will talk badly about me or African Americans in front of them. I just fear so many things when it comes to her and my children. I put nothing past her. That is why, if I can help it, she will never be alone with my children. I don't think my soul could rest knowing my children were alone with her. I don't even like being alone with her. You have no idea how passionate I am about this issue. Those are going to be my innocent babies, and I will give my life to make sure they do not experience an ounce of what I went through from his family. Any birthday parties, vacations, or days at Chuck E. Cheese, you better believe I will be there. And let me say this again, my husband supports my decision 110 percent.

Some of you may think that I am being a little harsh, but, ladies, put yourself in my shoes and walk around in them for six years. Know who I am dealing with here. This isn't a mother-in-law who's a little jealous that I took her son from her. This isn't a mother-in-law who's a control freak. And this isn't a mother-in-law who's always in your business. This is a person who wouldn't allow me in her home for the first three years of my relationship with her son because of the color of my skin. This is the most manipulative person I know (keep reading, you'll see). This is a person who doesn't like me because I am "black" and had no compunctions about letting me and my husband know it for years. For the past six years, she showed me what kind of person she truly is and what kind of heart she has. Trust me, harsh would be not allowing her to see our children at all; I am being reasonable.

I won't tell all of you to follow in my footsteps if you are in this situation. But I will tell you to follow your gut. If your gut tells you it is okay to have her babysit while you and your man go to the movies, then fine. If your soul is at ease with that, then go for it. On the other hand, if your gut tells you that you're not ready to leave your children alone with her, then don't. But don't forget to talk it over with your man. Let him know how you feel about this issue. Honestly, that's all I did with my husband. I told my husband about how I felt way before we were engaged. I knew that I wouldn't be comfortable leaving my children with her a long time ago. My husband understood fully how I felt because, by this point, he didn't quite trust her either. My husband would tell me he never realized, growing up, how racist his mother was until he started dating me; he saw a side of her he said he didn't know existed. And that side he doesn't trust, so he definitely understands where I was coming from.

My advice to you is to follow your gut; it's as simple as that. My husband tells me "you're going to be the mother, it's your call." Boy, I love that he says that. It's true, you are the mother, and she and everyone else has to respect the decisions you make about your children. Everything from whose house your children can and cannot go to, to what they can and cannot receive for Christmas (for example, no toy guns for Christmas, thanks). Those are your innocent babies, and they should not be exposed to anything unhealthy, even if it's their racist grandmother.

Who knows, it may just take you some time to build the trust you need in her to leave your children alone with her. I may not feel the way I feel forever. I know one thing; she has many, many years of proving she can be trusted by me. I honestly do not know what she could do to make me trust her because I feel she has ruined any chance of a friendship, or any sort of relationship between us. But for you, only time will tell. However, remember she has to prove she can be trusted. Don't think just because she is grandma and these are her grandchildren, she is harmless. I don't know about you, but I would be a fool to think that. I know better. But even though they say that children have a way of bringing out the best in people, I would have to see it to believe it when it comes to her.

Just be very attentive. Watch how she or any of his family members treats your children. Sit back and pretend that you're not paying attention, but pay very close attention. And you make the final decision about whether you like what you see or not. Remember, you are the mother, and they have to respect your decisions.

5

❖

You Must **Forgive**

You must be wondering how my husband and I made it through all the drama from his mother while we were dating. Well, it took a lot of prayer. Anyone who knew the situation was praying for us—my mom, friends, and the co-ed softball team my future husband and I played on. Even random people prayed for us. Prayer is powerful and it can change the most impossible situations. My husband and I would, of course, pray for a change in the hearts of his family members toward us being together, but our main prayer was for our relationship. We'd pray for God to give us strength to look past all the ignorance and negativity thrown at us from his family. And, thank God, we made it!

When it came to my own personal prayer, I would pray for God to help me forgive his mother for all the hurt and pain she caused me. Forgiving is so important for three crucial reasons: One, we must forgive to be forgiven by God. Matthew 6:14 says, "For if you forgive others for their transgressions, your heavenly Father will also forgive you." (New American Standard Bible)

So, if you do something terrible and you ask for God to forgive you for it, you must first forgive others who have hurt you.

After I forgave her, I prayed for God to help me totally forgive her. I wanted him to cleanse my heart of any grudges or ill feelings I held toward her. To forgive someone is not to hold a grudge against him or her. You can't totally forgive someone and still throw things she has done to you back in her face; that's not forgiveness.

When you forgive someone, you have to totally let go of all the wrong she (or he) has done to you. Don't get me wrong, forgiving someone doesn't mean you have to trust him or her. Take me for example, I forgave my husband's mother a long time ago for all the hurt and pain she has cause me and my husband, but I do not trust her for all that she has done to us. Plus, she has not given me any reason why I can trust her.

In a letter that I wrote to her, after my husband and I got married, I let her know that I don't hate her or hold anything against her. But I told her that I cannot trust her because of my memories of the past and the fact that she cannot give me a sincere apology to let me know she was wrong and feels bad for what she's done to me. Yes, I forgive her, hold no grudges toward her, and I know God knows my heart, but, in order for us to have some sort of relationship (because I am married to her son), I would need for her to give me a sincere apology. There's no way I could trust her enough to have meaningful conversations with her or even go to lunch with her when she feels that I don't need a sincere apology. She feels that everything she has done to me is perfectly fine.

Don't get me wrong, she has apologized to me; actually twice, but they were both forced and very fake. The first apology came after I had to pretty much ask for it, and, when I did, she almost jumped out of her skin as if I had cursed at her or something. She said, "*Apology?*" as if she wanted to say, "Apology for what?" She went on to say, "Well, I'm sorry if I did anything, Im sorry." Thank God I can laugh about it now because that day I was very insulted and more than angry. My husband wasn't there when the "apology" went down, but I told him I knew in my heart that her apology was not sincere.

See, I also prayed that, if his mother ever gave me an apology, God would bring peace to my heart. The peace that I would feel would be a confirmation that she was truly sorry. Well, I have yet to receive peace about any of her apologies. And get this, a couple of weeks after her so called "sincere" apology, she and my husband ended up getting into an argument, and she kept telling him that her apology to me was sincere. So, my husband finally asked her if she even knew what she had apologized for and she said, "No! I just apologized because she wanted me to." How can someone apologize *sincerely* about something and not even know what it is? I don't get it.

The second apology came after she wrote me the most manipulating letter as a response to my letter to her. And just to add, in my letter I told her that, when God places it in her heart to give me a sincere apology, I would accept it. Well, you will read more about her response to my letter later, but I got everything else *but* an apology from it. Her letter really hurt me, but I chose to ignore everything she said in the letter because it's obvious her eyes are shielded. I don't think she wants to see all the wrong she has done to my husband and me. She wants to continue portraying herself as this nice, innocent person.

After receiving her letter, my husband had to call her and convince her that the way she had treated me for six years was racist and wrong. She ended up getting frustrated (truth hurts) and yelled, "Fine, if that's what you want to hear; I'm sorry for being racist to her." That, to her, is a "sincere" apology. I ended up giving her the benefit of the doubt (for the umpteenth time) because I finally gave up on getting a sincere apology from her. I realized that I can't make her apologize for something that she feels she has not done; that is beyond my control.

These days, I pray the shield is lifted from her eyes, so she can see all the hurt that she has caused; then maybe she will feel compelled to heal open wounds—if not for my sake, then for the sake of her future grandchildren and my husband. But when the shield is lifted, I pray that God comforts her heart for what will be revealed to her. The truth will hurt.

My advice to you is to pray to God to help you forgive his mother or any other person in his family who caused you pain. Ask God to cleanse your heart and soul of any ill feelings you may have toward her. But remember, if she hasn't sincerely apologized to you, then you do not have to trust her. Yes, you have to forgive her … not for her, but for you.

In saying that, the second reason you should forgive her is for yourself. When you don't forgive someone, you carry such a heavy burden in your heart and soul. Before I asked God to help me forgive her, I use to walk into her home angry, trying to avoid her, not smiling, and just feeling miserable. It was exhausting and stressful. I would leave her house with a migraine because I was so tense. It took a lot of energy and hard work (at least for me) trying not to totally dislike her or to hold a grudge against her. I am not a person to hold grudges or to hate someone. I mean, look at all the times I gave her the benefit of the doubt. Peace, love, and happiness are what I yearn for, not confusion and drama.

When I asked God to help me forgive her and to cleanse my heart of all the ill feelings I had toward her, I felt as if a ton of bricks had been lifted off my shoulders. I felt happy and free. I could smile again because I had been freed of the burden that not forgiving someone can bring upon you. I let go of all the grudges I held on to and moved on.

For so long I let all the things she had done to me affect and change who I was. You will hear me constantly tell you to never let who she is or what she has done to you change who you are. Now I go to her home carefree, full of peace, and with my head up.

Realize that, when you don't forgive someone, you don't hurt that person, you hurt yourself. You become bitter and even angry. When you choose to forgive, you choose to let go of the anger and resentment. Once you let it go, you will be able to grab hold of peace and happiness.

The third reason you should forgive his mother is to release the control she has over you. Yes, she is controlling you if you haven't forgiven her yet. If you don't forgive her, she has the power to make you miserable. I walked into her home angry and miserable as a result of her control over me. And I'm sure she liked the fact that she had the power to make me miserable. Well, not anymore. God helped me forgive her and he helped me move on. As I said before, I walk into her home now happy and unbothered by her.

If she never gives me the sincere apology I deserve, it's okay. I will still live my life happily because, by the grace of God, I have forgiven her. So, even if you haven't receive an apology yet, forgive her. Not for her sake but for your spiritual and emotional well-being. Don't think forgiving her means you condone what she has done to you. It will just help you to not be so consumed and taken over by all the wrong that she has done to you, which will eventually cause you to become bitter, angry, and revengeful. In addition, forgiving her doesn't mean you have to trust her. You trust her when she apologizes and earns your trust. And that may take a lifetime.

6

❖

Be Respectful and Kind at All Times

This is the most important chapter in this book. If you don't take any of my previous advice, please take the advice I give in this chapter. Always, let me repeat, *always* show respect and kindness to his mother. Never let her make you stoop to her level.

I know this may be hard to follow, especially when she is so disrespectful to you, but you have to respect her; she is and will always be his mother. Also, another biggie is to never say anything disrespectful about her in front of your man.

Don't let me fool you; I had my break-down moment also. One time I said something really rude to my husband about his mother. He had called and told me that his mother was telling him that the reason he hangs out with me and my family is because he thinks he's black! Anyway, I was just so annoyed by her and her comments, every other day, that I said, "She's crazy!" Oops. My husband didn't call me out on it or get upset at my comment, but, immediately after I said it, I felt horrible. We finished our conversation and said our good-byes and hung up. I was so bothered by what I had said to him that I ended up calling him right back to tell him how sorry I was. After that, I never said anything bad about his mother to him.

I certainly understand that you may need to vent sometimes about the situation, but he is not the person to vent to about his own mother. There would be times that my husband would be angry and vent to me about his mother, but I just listened. I would never throw in my two cents about her. I would just let him do all the talking.

Never assume that it's okay to repeat what your man is saying while he is fuming about his family. Know your boundaries, and know "the rule." You know—that rule that says, "I can say whatever I want to say about my family and friends, but you'd better not say it." That's why I would never jump in and offer my two cents while he was ranting about his mother. I knew "the rule." She is your man's mother, and he has the right to say whatever he wants about her, but you don't have the right to repeat it.

When you think that you are about to disrespect her or make a rude comment about her, always remember this: when you make disrespectful comments to him about his mother, you are actually disrespecting him, not her.

Of course, hearing certain things my husband's mother would say about me would make me angry, and I would want to retaliate and say nasty things to or about her. But never did I stoop to her level. I was always the bigger person and showed her respect; no matter what she had said or done to me. Unlike her, I have too much respect for my husband to do that.

This is what my mother-in-law failed to realize—that every time she disrespected me, to him or in front of him, she was really hurting and disrespecting him, not me. I was the woman her son was in love with, but she didn't care. She would still talk down about me to him as if it was nothing. She never had enough respect for him to keep her negative, racist comments to herself. This is another reason he doesn't trust her to this day. She showed him for years how much respect she truly had for him.

Another reason to stay respectful and kind to her is so she will have nothing to hold against you (you've heard that a lot, I know). Let her be the bad one by herself. Never give her anything to use against you. If you were to ask my husband's mother, "Why don't you like Jetta?"

she couldn't say she doesn't like me because I disrespected her, her home, or her family. She could never say I was mean to her or gave her attitude or fought with her. She has no justifiable reason not to like me because I never gave her one. She tries so hard to tell me it's not because I'm black, but she doesn't realize she is making it obvious that it is because I'm black. Because I gave her nothing to dislike me for and I never stooped to her level, she looks like the bad one in the situation, which, in reality, she is.

My husband and his parents did not talk for two months after we were married. This is when I wrote my letter to reach out to her. I told her that I would love to start over with her, but, in order for me to do that, I would need a sincere apology from her. Let me tell you, she wrote me back the most manipulative letter I have ever read. She flipped everything to make herself look like the victim. In her letter, she wrote that I had been mean to her and basically called me the racist one because I don't like the color of *her* skin (funny). She even had the nerve to say that I owed her an apology, and the apology needed to be whole hearted because, if it wasn't, it would just cause more pain.

Are you kidding me? I give her an apology? *That's funny.* Oh, and she told me that, if I loved my husband, I would bring him closer to his family instead of separating him from them. Her eyes are so shielded, she can't see that the separation occurred because of the way she treated my husband and me for years, not because of me.

So, I let my husband read this ridiculous letter, and he was fuming by the time he was finished. He ended up calling her and asking her what the heck was she talking about. All she could do was stutter and say she meant for those parts to be for him not me. Yeah, she was saying that *he* didn't like her skin color (which is the same as his—white). Does that make sense to you? Well it still doesn't make sense to me. I just figured she was trying to make something up (as usual) so she could look like the victim and wouldn't have to admit her wrongs and apologize to me. Plus, she knows that she truly has no valid reason to have treated me the way she did for so long, except for the "real" reason—my race. In the end, just like all of her other ridiculous excuses, this letter made her look plain foolish.

My point is, when you show her nothing but respect and give her nothing to use against you, she will either say nothing (which is what my husband's mother should have done) or she will look ridiculous in the pursuit of trying to find something to use against you. I know it's hard, but continue ignoring her ignorance and continue to be respectful to her.

Now, let's say you have already stooped to her level and let her have a piece of your mind. Or, she has done or said so many mean things about you or to you that you now resent her. Well, it's okay. This can be fixed. From this point on, you will be the bigger person.

First, you should write her a letter to say you're sorry. I know it's easier said than done, but I bet she hasn't apologized to you yet. So be the first to say you're sorry. You don't even have to hand her the letter, you can mail it. But I do think you should hand write it. Letters that are hand written are more personal than typed or e-mailed messages.

In the letter, don't really get into what made you angry or what made you say or do whatever you said or did that was disrespectful. Only tell her that you're sorry for what you did to disrespect her. Also tell her that you would love (or like) to have a better relationship with her. Tell her that you cannot change the past, but you are willing to move on and let it go if she is. And ask her to accept your apology. Add whatever else you want in the letter, but don't go backwards and start talking about the past. This letter, hopefully, is the start of a new beginning. One more thing—if you're asking her to forgive you and you truly want to move on, make sure you are truly sorry. Before you write the letter, pray to God to help you forgive her.

After writing the letter, you have to practice what you preach. If you say you want to move on, then do so. Don't keep bringing up the bad things she has said or done to you. And don't wait for her to respond to the letter to start your new attitude. She may not respond to your letter, and she might even pretend she never received it, but you know you wrote it and you meant your words. So go ahead and let it all go.

And if she doesn't accept your apology or she doesn't respond, or, like my husband's mother, writes you back a manipulative and insulting response, don't worry about it and don't respond to her. If she does take my mother-in-law's approach to your letter, all she is trying to do is make you angry, to make you go back to the old you. She will try a lot of things to make you fall backwards to disrespect her again because she doesn't want to be the only bad one in this situation. Don't fall for it; ignore her ignorance.

Remember, you did the right thing by writing the apology letter. Plus, you're going to be doing an even better thing when you start to make kind gestures and do kind things toward her.

The next time you see her, have a positive attitude and say, "Hi, how are you?" She may think you're crazy because all of a sudden you're being extra nice to her, but don't worry about what she thinks from this point on. You can't live your life based on what she thinks.

Don't be afraid to offer some sort of kind gesture whenever you see her. Flash her a friendly smile or try to say one nice thing every time you see her. If she has on pretty earrings, tell her that they're pretty. If she has on a cute shirt or cute shoes, tell her. Now, I know this is something that will take time, but keep it in mind whenever you do see her. And remember to be sincere in your gestures. Even though my attempts to be kind to my mother-in-law has yet to work, I still believe that if you are sincere in your effort to be nice to someone despite their treatment of you, I think you nurture a positive feeling within yourself, and you might also inspire a positive feeling in the other person. This could work for you, so stay sincerely kind to his mother.

For her birthday, give her a card. If you don't want to hand it to her, that's fine, just mail it. The thought is what counts. One birthday, my husband and I bought his mother a little birthday cake; just that simple. All she could do was say thank you.

For Christmas, buy her a gift. And don't just go through the motions of getting her any old gift; get her something that you know she likes. Getting her something that she likes shows that you care and that you pay attention. My husband's mother has a lot of angels around the house, so one Christmas I bought her a snow globe with an angel in the middle. She also loves hazelnut coffee, so I bought her some.

When you're invited to dinner or a party, always bring dessert or a bottle of wine; don't go empty handed. If you see her in the kitchen cooking, ask her if she needs any help. What's the worst she could say? No? If you think about it, it's not that hard. I guess I should say, don't think about it, just do it.

And always have a smile on your face. Walk into her house with your head up; you have no reason to hang your head. Don't let what she has done to you and what kind of person she is change who you are. If you had a boyfriend who had a mother who adored you, you would do all these nice things for her naturally because you would think she was worth it. When someone is nice to you, it makes you want to be nice to them. In this situation, you have to force yourself to be nice to someone who isn't so nice to you, but you can do it.

When you do kind things, she can't do anything but accept them. If she doesn't accept your kind acts, don't sweat it. You did your part and you made the effort, but don't let her discourage you from being nice. Continue to send birthday cards and Christmas gifts; be the bigger person.

Doing nice things will also catch her off guard; she won't expect it at all. One New Years we showed up at his parents' house, and I brought her a gift (more hazelnut coffee!). When I walked into the house, I told her I'd brought her a New Years gift, and I put it on the kitchen counter. She didn't even make an attempt to open it. She just kept avoiding it until my husband said, "Aren't you going to open your gift?" I caught her so off guard with my gift that she tried to say she didn't know it was for her. I don't see how that's possible because I looked her in her eyes and said, "I brought you a gift." She said she thought it was for his father. Even his father said, "No, Jetta brought that for you." All she could do was open it and say thank you.

I will always continue to be kind to her. As I said before, I can't let what kind of person she has been to me and what she has done to me change me into a mean, bitter person. Plus, the person who matters most—your man—will love you even more when he notices your newfound respect for his mother. He will also see that you are putting forth the effort to improve the situation. My husband has always told me that he notices and appreciates every effort I make and he appreciates how I have always been respectful to his mother. Remember, good always prevails

7

❖

How Are Things Today?

I'm sure your wondering how things are today with my mother-in law. Well, my husband and I are happy; mainly because we made it through all the negativity and ignorance thrown at use from his mother and a few others in his family. Boy, was it hard, but we made it.

Everything got a little better with his parents after the second "fake" apology. Well, at least now they are talking. As I said before, I gave up on getting a sincere apology and just gave her the benefit of the doubt. We go visit his parents once or twice a month. And when we go, we only stay about an hour before my husband gives me the "are-you-ready-to-go" look.

My husband's father is making huge efforts to prove to my husband and I that he accepts me … well us. After the second apology, we were invited to dinner at their house, and his father made me feel extremely welcome. He made conversation with me, asking me about my job, and making little jokes. Little things like that matter to me because it shows he wants to get to know me as his son's wife. Every time we visit, my husband's father always talks to me and greets me with a kiss on the cheek. He just seems truly genuine these days.

On the other hand, my husband and his mother hardly talk. When they do talk, it's civil conversation, but he'd rather make a phone call and talk to his father. As I said before, the harsh things she has said to him and the way she has treated us for loving each other have damaged his trust for her.

I wish I had a better ending to tell you about my current relationship with my mother-in-law, but I don't. I still don't trust her because she still has yet to humble herself and apologize to me sincerely. I have told her that I do not trust her and she has told me that she respects my feelings. She also told me that she hopes that one day I will get to know her. She says she hopes my feelings will change and I might start trusting her. But she barely talks to me when we visit. She only says, "Hi, Jetta" or just plain, "Hello." She never tries to start random conversation with me or ask me anything about myself. I don't understand how she expects me to get to know her and build a trust with her when she doesn't even talk to me. I have tried for years to get to know her—to no avail. In return I receive only manipulation and excuses for her behavior toward me. Now I think it's her turn to put forth the effort to make me feel comfortable around her. It's time for her to prove to me that she can be trusted. Until then, it is what it is, and I'm okay with the way things are. I have done my part in the past, and I continue to do my part; that's what matters to me.

I do little things now to show her that I am still open to her, like sending her inspirational e-mails and making it a point to remember her birthday. I actually sent her a happy birthday text for her birthday recently and I didn't get a thank you reply back. But that's okay; I did the right thing. I know the things that I do are simple and small, but at least I'm doing something, which is way more than what she gives me.

I take this entire situation as a life lesson not to treat people badly when you don't know them. When my husband and I started to date, I'm sure his mother thought our relationship was just a fling. She probably thought that her son dating a black girl was just a phase he was going through. But look at us now; we're married. I am now her daughter-in-law, and look at all the horrible memories I have of her. Look at how she has treated me. I am the mother of her future grandchildren, and what good do I have to tell them of her? It's a truly sad and unfortunately reality. I definitely learned to never judge or treat anyone badly without getting to know them. You never know what God has planned for you and that person. Hebrews 13:2 says, "Be not forgetful to entertain strangers: for thereby some have entertained angels unawares." (King James Version)

I hope you enjoyed the book, and I hope you don't feel so alone in this situation now. Yes, there are others who are or who have been in the same predicament you're in. My goal for this book was to help women in this unfortunate situation gain some insight on how to deal with it. Remember, to always show her respect and ask God to help you forgive her. So, I hope you're more prepared to date the other color and his mother.

A Recap of the Most Important Things To Remember

When dealing with *her* ...

✓ Don't let his mother manipulate you into giving her information that's truly none of her business. Give her information you want her to know when you want her to know it.

✓ Don't fall for her fakeness; you will end up hurt and extremely disappointed. She is only genuine and sincere after she gives you the apology you deserve.

✓ Never let her see you and your boyfriend/husband fight.

✓ Laugh her off when she tries to make you jealous of another woman.

✓ Keep your personal information personal. You never know when she could be listening, watching, or researching you.

✓ Don't think that, just because she is your children's grandmother, she is harmless. I do not agree with totally keeping her from her grandchildren; but I will say, follow your gut.

✓ Be kind and respectful to her at all times.

✓ Last, but certainly not least, *forgive* her for all the hurt she has caused you. Forgive her not for her, but for yourself (and your man).

When dealing with *him* …

- ✓ Don't blame him for the faults of his mother.
- ✓ Make sure he is standing up for you, but understand *his* way of standing up for you.
- ✓ Cut him some slack and understand his circumstances. This is his mother he is battling so that he can be with you.
- ✓ When he does stand up for you, tell him how much you appreciate it.
- ✓ Never talk negatively about his mother in front of him. You're only disrespecting him—not her.

When dealing with *yourself* …

Never let who she is or what she has done to you change who you are as a person. Don't let these unfortunate circumstances turn you into a bitter, revengeful and unforgiving person. Continue to be the sweet, kind, caring, and down-to-earth person you truly are.

Notes